BURT FRANKLIN: BIBLIOGRAPHY & REFERENCE SERIES 381
Selected Essays in History, Economics, & Social Science 193

CAPTAIN JOHNSON:
A BIBLIOGRAPHY

By the Same Author.

THE PIRATE'S WHO'S WHO.
MY PIRATE LIBRARY.

A BIBLIOGRAPHY

OF THE WORKS OF

CAPT. CHARLES JOHNSON

BY

PHILIP GOSSE

BURT FRANKLIN
NEW YORK

Published by LENOX HILL Pub. & Dist. Co. (Burt Franklin)
235 East 44th St., New York, N.Y. 10017
Originally Published: 1927
Reprinted: 1970
Printed in the U.S.A.

S.B.N.: 8337-13914
Library of Congress Card Catalog No.: 72-127189
Burt Franklin: Bibliography and Reference Series 381
Selected Essays in History, Economics, and Social Science 193

THIS WORK IS

DEDICATED

TO

MY MANY FRIENDS
AMONGST THE LONDON BOOKSELLERS

Blackbeard the Pirate

Second edition, 1724.

PREFACE

IN the following pages an attempt has been made to describe and fully collate the various editions and reprints that have appeared during the last two hundred years of the two works attributed to Captain Charles Johnson. They are the " General History of the Pyrates " and the " General History of the Highwaymen."

The former was first published in London in 1724 by Rivington, and is always known as the first edition. Quite recently my friend Mr. Frank Maggs called my attention to an entry in " The History of Printing in America," by Isaiah Thomas, LL.D., Albany, N.Y., 1874.

On p. 397, Vol. II., appears the following entry:

" 1723. Johnson: Capt. Charles. Gen. Hist of Pyrates from their first rise and settlement in the Island of Providence to the present time, etc. NEW YORK. Printed by Wm. Bradford. 1723."

Nothing more is said and no collation given.

This is followed on page 399 by:

" 1724. 2nd Edition. New York. Printed by Bradford."

Every endeavour has been made to trace a copy of either of these editions. The Librarians of the chief American Libraries have been written to, but not one of them has heard of, and still less seen, a copy.

I can find no mention of it in any other work of reference, and feel justified in still describing the earlier of the 1724 London Editions as the first.

Johnson's second book, the "History of the Highwaymen" (London, 1734), is really a reissue of Captain Alexander Smith's "History of the Lives and Robberies of the Most Notorious Highwaymen," first published in 1711, and which ran into several editions. To this Johnson added several of his pirates, and many engravings. This handsome folio comes into the market from time to time, and a sound copy fetches about thirty pounds or more.

No copy of the first (Rivington) edition has come up for sale for several years: in fact the only copy besides my own two that I have been able to trace in England is one in the Bodleian Library at Oxford.

Wherever possible, my collaborators and I have made collations from the actual books, generally in my own possession: but in the case of copies that only exist in the larger American Libraries we have relied on the never-failing kindness of the Librarians of these Institutions for full particulars.

Only in a few cases have we heard of editions and not been able to trace a copy.

For example, there is a self-styled "fifth edition," the only record of which we have been able to find is a reproduction of the title-page shown in Messrs. Simpkin, Marshall, Hamilton, Kent and Co.'s publication "Pirates" (No. 56) with illustrations by Lovat Fraser.

This seems to have been a very abbreviated travesty of Johnson's original history, but was "adorned with twenty Beautiful Cuts" and was published in London in 1735 by A. Betteswood, E. Hitch and others.

Certain other editions we have heard of but have been unable to trace, which have not been included in our list, but which are noted here. They are: a French translation of the "Pirates" published at Utrecht, 1725; the "Highwaymen" published by T. Avis at Birmingham, 1742; another edition of the same with coloured plates, published by Smeeton, N.D., similar to Hodge's edition (No. 23).

This bibliography, although but a small one, has been a labour of no small degree, and any credit that it possesses is due to the untiring energy and unflagging enthusiasm of the late Frank Wood, my collaborator and friend. Two years ago young Wood came up to London to realize his ambition in becoming a bookseller. His industry and energy had started him well on the road to success when a sudden illness brought his promising career to a close. By his death I lost not only a fellow enthusiast about books, but a very good friend.

This preface cannot close without a few words of thanks, however inadequate, to all those who have so kindly and so patiently answered innumerable letters of enquiry, or helped by the loan of books for collation.

I particularly wish to thank Mr. Charles F. D. Beldon, Director of the Public Library of the City of Boston; Mr. Robert O. Schad, Assistant Curator, and Mr. Willard O. Waters, head cataloguer, of the Henry E. Huntington Library, California; the Superintendent of the Reading Room, the Library of Congress, Washington; Mr. Francis S. Parks, of Chestnut Hill, Massachusetts; Mr. William Maxwell Cooper, of the National Library of Scotland, Edinburgh; and Mr. H. Guppy, Director of the John Rylands Library, Manchester.

I must also thank my old friend Mr. Francis Edwards, of Marylebone, for all the help and advice he has given me. My thanks are also due to Mr. W. T. Spencer for the loan of a volume for collation.

Lastly, I must express my indebtedness to Mr. A. E. Davies, of the London Library, for all the care and trouble he has taken to make this bibliography, if not complete, at all events as free from errors as care can make it.

PHILIP GOSSE.

CONTENTS

JOHNSON BIBLIOGRAPHY

B. cole sculp.

Blackbeard the Pirate

First edition, 1724.

1724.

1. A GENERAL / HISTORY / OF THE / ROBBERIES AND MURDERS / OF THE MOST NOTORIOUS / PYRATES, / and also / Their Policies, Discipline and Government, / From their first Rise and Settlement in the Island / of Providence, in 1717, to the present Year 1724. / With / The remarkable Actions / and Adventures of the two Fe- / male Pyrates, Mary Read and Anne Bonny. / To which is prefix'd / An Account of the famous Captain Avery and his Com- / panions; with the Manner of his Death in England. / The Whole digested into the following Chapters: /

Chap. I. Of Captain Avery.
II. The Rise of the Pyrates.
III. Of Captain Martel.
IV. Of Captain Bonnet.
V. Of Captain Thatch.
VI. Of Captain Vane.
VII. Of Captain Rackam.
VIII. Of Captain England.
IX. Of Captain Davis.
X. Of Captain Roberts.
XI. Of Captain Worley.
XII. Of Captain Lowther.
XIII. Of Captain Low.
XIV. Of Captain Evans.

And their several Crews. / To which is added, / A short Abstract of the Statute and Civil Law, in / Relation to Pyracy. / (*rule*) / By Captain Charles Johnson. / (*rule*) / London, Printed for Ch. Rivington at the Bible and Crown in St. / Paul's Church-Yard, J. Lacy at the Ship near the Temple-Gate, and / J. Stone next the Crown Coffee-house the back of Greys-Inn, 1724. /

Octavo.   Present copy measures $7\frac{1}{8}$ ins. by $4\frac{1}{2}$ ins.

Signatures.—(A) (11 leaves), B to U in eights.

Pagination.—Title, verso blank, preface 6 pp. (unnumbered), contents 14 pp. (unnumbered), pp. 17 to 320. There are 3 engraved plates, by B. Cole, facing pp. 86, 117, and 202; the last two are folding plates.

P. 80 is misnumbered 90, and p. 206 reads 06.   O4 is mis-signed O3.   First Edition.

1724.

2. A GENERAL / HISTORY / OF THE / PYRATES, / from / Their first Rise and Settlement in the˙ Island of / Providence, to the present Time. / With the remarkable Actions and Adventures of the two Female Pyrates / Mary Read and Anne Bonny; / Contain'd in the following Chapters, /

Introduction.	IX. Of Capt. Roberts.
Chap. I. Of Capt. Avery.	X. Of Capt. Anstis.
II. Of Capt. Martel.	XI. Of Capt. Worley.
III. Of Capt. Teach.	XII. Of Capt. Lowther.
IV. Of Capt. Bonnet.	XIII. Of Capt. Low.
V. Of Capt. England.	XIV. Of Capt. Evans.
VI. Of Capt. Vane.	XV. Of Capt. Phillips.
VII. Of Capt. Rackam.	XVI. Of Capt. Spriggs.
VIII. Of Capt. Davis.	And their several Crews.

To which is added, / A short Abstract of the Statute and Civil / Law, in Relation to Pyracy. / (*rule*) / The second Edition, with considerable Additions / (*rule*) / By Captain Charles Johnson. / (*rule*) / London: / Printed for, and sold by T. Warner, at the Black-Boy in Pater- / Noster-Row, 1724. /

Octavo.   Present copy measures 7¾ ins. by 4¾ ins.

Signatures.—(A) (10 leaves), B to Cc in eights, Dd (6 leaves).

Pagination.—Title, verso blank, preface 8 pp. (unnumbered), list of contents 10 pp. (unnumbered), pp. 17 to 427, p. (428) contains an advertisement of a forthcoming book. There are 3 engraved plates, by B. Cole, facing pp. 70, 157, and 259; the last two are folding plates.

The 9 has been dropped from p. 92.

The plate of Blackbeard has been altered to accord with the description in the text, the one in the first edition being incorrect.

P. 329 reads 229, the 9 is missing from p. 349, and p. 414 reads 14.

There was a second issue, by Robert Knaplock, of this edition. It has the same title-page, but is concluded by 16 pp. of advertisements under his name, the sheets signed A and B in fours.

1725.

3. A GENERAL / HISTORY / OF THE / PYRATES, / from / Their first Rise and Settlement in the Island of / Providence, to the present Time. / With the remarkable Actions and Adventures of the two Female Pyrates / Mary Read and Anne Bonny; / Contain'd in the following Chapters, /

<table>
<tr><td>Introduction.</td><td>IX. Of Capt. Roberts.</td></tr>
<tr><td>Chap. I. Of Capt. Avery.</td><td>X. Of Capt. Anstis.</td></tr>
<tr><td>II. Of Capt. Martel.</td><td>XI. Of Capt. Worley.</td></tr>
<tr><td>III. Of Capt. Teach.</td><td>XII. Of Capt. Lowther.</td></tr>
<tr><td>IV. Of Capt. Bonnet.</td><td>XIII. Of Capt. Low.</td></tr>
<tr><td>V. Of Capt. England.</td><td>XIV. Of Capt. Evans.</td></tr>
<tr><td>VI. Of Capt. Vane.</td><td>XV. Of Capt. Phillips.</td></tr>
<tr><td>VII. Of Capt. Rackam.</td><td>XVI. Of Capt. Spriggs.</td></tr>
<tr><td>VIII. Of Capt. Davis.</td><td>XVII. Of Capt. Smith.</td></tr>
</table>

And their several Crews. / To which is added, / A short Abstract of the Statute and Civil / Law, in Relation to Pyracy. / (*rule*) / The Third Edition. / (*rule*) / By Captain Charles Johnson. / (*rule*) / London: / Printed for, and sold by T. Warner, at the Black-Boy in Pater- / Noster-Row. 1725. /

Octavo.   Present copy measures $7\frac{3}{4}$ ins. by $4\frac{3}{4}$ ins.

Signatures.—(A) (10 leaves), B to Cc in eights, Dd (6 leaves).

Pagination.—Title, verso blank, preface 8 pp. (unnumbered), list of contents 10 pp. (unnumbered), pp. 17 to 427, p. (428) contains an advertisement of a forthcoming book. There are 3 engraved plates, by B. Cole, facing pp. 71, 157, and 259; the last two are folding plates.

The 9's have been dropped from pp. 289 and 349, p. 329 reads 229, and p. 414 reads 14.   P4 is missigned P3.

1725.

4. A GENERAL / HISTORY / OF / PYRATES, / Their / Robberies and Murders, / as also / Their Policies, Discipline and Government. / From their first Rise and Settlement in the Island of / Providence, to the present Year, 1724. / With / The remarkable Actions and Adventures of the two Fe- / male Pyrates, Mary Read and Anne Bonny. / To which is prefix'd / An Account of the famous Captain Avery / and his Companions; with the Manner of his Death / in England. / The whole digested into the following Chapters. /

Chap. I. Of Capt. Avery,	VIII. Of Capt. England,
II. The Rise of the Pyrates,	IX. Of Capt. Davis,
III. Of Capt. Martel,	X. Of Capt. Roberts,
IV. Of Capt. Bonnet,	XI. Of Capt. Worley,
V. Of Capt. Thatch,	XII. Of Capt. Lowther,
VI. Of Capt. Vane,	XIII. Of Capt. Low,
VII. Of Capt. Rackam,	XIV. Of Capt. Evans.

And their several Crews. / To which is added, / A short Abstract of the Statute and Civil / Law, in Relation to Pyracy. / (*rule*) / By Capt. Charles Johnson. / (*rule*) / Dublin: Printed by J. Watts, and sold opposite / the Watch-House, on the North-Side of College-Green, / MDCCXXV. /

Duodecimo. The present copy measures 6¾ ins. by 4 ins.

Signatures.—(A) to Z in fours.

Pagination.—Title, verso blank, preface 6 pp. (unnumbered), pp. (1) to 248. There is an engraved frontispiece portrait of Blackbeard reproduced from the first edition, depicting him with the short thick beard instead of the long plaited one which he actually did wear, and which appears in the illustrations to the subsequent English editions.

The present copy has signature T bound in twice.

1725.

5. HISTORIE / DER ENGELSCHE / ZEE-ROOVERS, /
Beginnende met de Geschiedenisse van / Capiteyn Avery,
en zyne / Makkers. A°. 1692. / Behelsende een Verhaal van
hunne Zee- / Rooveryen, Moorderyen, Wreedhe- / den, en
Mishandelingen, &c. / Waar by gevoegd is het Leeven van /
Mary Read en Anne Bonney, / Twee Zee-Roovende Vrou-
wen. / In het Engelsch Beschreeven, door / Capiteyn Charles
Johnson, / En in het Nederduytsch overgezet, door / Robert
Hennebo / Verceird met Kopere Plaaten. / Eerste Deel. /
(*ornament*) / Tot Amsterdam, / By Hermanus Uytwerf,
1725. /

Octavo. The British Museum copy measures 6⅜ ins. by
3⅜ ins. Mr. F. S. Parks' (of Massachusetts) copy measures
6⅞ ins. by 3¾ ins.

Signatures.—(Vol. I.) A to Z in eights, (Vol II.) Aa to Yy
in eights.

Pagination.—Engraved half-title, verso blank, title (Vol. I.),
verso blank, pp. 1 to 368, title (Vol. II.), verso blank, pp. 369
to 720. There are seven engraved plates.

The two volumes are bound in one, title of Vol. II. as in
Vol. I., substituting Tweede Deel for Eerste Deel. The end
of Vol. II. (p. 720) reads, " Eynde van het Eerste Deel."

The title is in black and red.

1725.

6. SCHAUPLATZ / DER ENGLISHEN / SEE-RAUBER, / Worinnen / Ihre Begebenheiten, Leben, Raubereyen und / grausame Thaten von der Zeit an da sie sich zuerst / auf der Insel Providentia niedergelassen, biss zu / unserer Zeit / Mit einem Auszug der Gesetze und / Ordannancen von Seeräuberey / Ausführlich zuerst in Englischer Sprache beschrieben / von / Capitaine Carl Johnsohn / Nachgehends im Frantzösischen, aus beyden Sprachen / aber ins Teutsch übersetzet aus beglaubten Urkunden continui- / ret, und mit Historisch-Geographischen Anmerckungen / Wie auch / einer Vorrede von der Seeräuberey der alten / und jetzigen Zeiten, vermehret / von / J.M.D. / (*long rule*) / Gosslar, / Verlegts Johann Christoph Konig, 1728 /

Octavo. The British Museum copy measures 6⅝ ins. by 4 ins.

Signatures.—a3 to d, A to Nn in eights.

Pagination.—Title, verso blank, dedication pp. i to viii, translator's preface pp. ix to lx, pp. 1 to 576. There is an engraved frontispiece.

The dedication and preface are signed Joachim Meier. The title is in red and black.

A translation of Vol. I. of Johnson's " History of the Pyrates."

7. *Vol. I.*   **1726.**

A GENERAL / HISTORY / OF THE / PYRATES, / from / Their first Rise and Settlement in the Island of / Providence, to the present Time. / With the remarkable Actions and Adventures of the two Female Pyrates / Mary Read and Anne Bonny; / Contain'd in the following Chapters, /

Introduction.	IX. Of Capt. Roberts.
Chap. I. Of Capt. Avery.	X. Of Capt. Anstis.
II. Of Capt. Martel.	XI. Of Capt. Worley.
III. Of Capt. Teach.	XII. Of Capt. Lowther.
IV. Of Capt. Bonnet.	XIII. Of Capt. Low.
V. Of Capt. England.	XIV. Of Capt. Evans.
VI. Of Capt. Vane.	XV. Of Capt. Phillips.
VII. Of Capt. Rackam.	XVI. Of Capt. Spriggs.
VIII. Of Capt. Davis.	XVII. Of Capt. Smith.

And their several Crews. / To which is added, / a short Abstract of the Statute and Civil / Law, in Relation to Pyracy. / (*rule*) / The Fourth Edition. / (*rule*) / Vol. I. / (*rule*) / By Captain Charles Johnson. / (*rule*) / London: / Printed for, and Sold by T. Woodward, at the Half-Moon, / over against St. Dunstan's Church, Fleet-Street. 1726. /

Signatures.—(A) (10 leaves), B to Ee in eights.

Pagination.—Title, verso blank, preface 8 pp. (unnumbered), list of contents 10 pp. (unnumbered), pp. 17 to 443, p. (444) blank. There are 3 engraved plates, by B. Cole, facing pp. 70, 157, and 259; the last two are folding plates.

P. 60 reads 90, p. 208 reads 108, p. 435 reads 434, pp. 438 and 439 read 436 and 437, pp. 442 and 443 read 438 and 439 and pp. 446 and 447 read 442 and 443.

7. *Vol. II.* **1726.**

THE / HISTORY / OF THE / PYRATES, / Containing the Lives of /

Captain Misson.	Captain Fly.
Captain Bowen.	Captain Howard.
Captain Kidd.	Captain Lewis.
Captain Tew.	Captain Cornelius.
Captain Halsey.	Captain Williams.
Captain White.	Captain Burgess.
Captain Condent.	Captain North.
Captain Bellamy.	

And their several Crews. / Intermix'd with a / Description of Magadoxa in Ethiopia; the natural Hatred / and Cruelty of the Inhabitants to all Whites; their Laws, Man- / ners, Customs, Government and Religion; With a particular / Account of the beautiful Tombs, / and their Ceremony / of guarding them, taken from Captain Beavis's Journal; and / that of a Molotto who belong'd to the said Captain, was taken by, and lived several Years with the Magadoxians. / To the Whole is added / An Appendix, which compleats the Lives of the first Volume, / corrects some Mistakes; and contains the Tryal and Execution / of the Pyrates at Providence, under Governor Rogers; with some other / necessary Insertions, which did not come to Hand till after the Publica- / tion of the first Volume, and which makes up what was defective Col- / lected from Journals of Pyrates, brought along by a Person who was ta- / ken by, and forc'd to live with them 12 Years; and from those of Com- / manders, who had fallen into their Hands, some of whom have per- / mitted their Names to be made use of, as a Proof of the Veracity of / what we have published. The Whole instructive and entertain- ing. / (*rule*) / Vol. II. / (*rule*) / By Captain Charles Johnson,

Author of Vol. I. / (*rule*) / *Omne tulit punctum, qui miscuit utile dulci.* Hor. / (*rule*) / London: / Printed for, and Sold by T. Woodward, at the Half-Moon, / over-against St. Dunstan's Church, Fleet-street. /

Signatures.—(A) [7 leaves—the title-page being (A2)], B to Dd in eights.

Pagination.—Title, verso blank, list of contents 12 pp. (unnumbered), pp. 1 to 413, pp. (414) to (416) publisher's advertisements. There is a folding frontispiece map of the coast of the " Middle of America."

Pp. 145 to 256 are wrongly numbered 161 to 272, otherwise the pagination is regular.

There is no date on the title-page of this first appearance of a second volume of Johnson's "Pyrates." The fact that it was first issued with the Fourth Edition of Vol. I. is proved by the appearance in the advertisements of Books printed for Tho. Woodward, at the end of Vol. II., of a notice advertising " The Fourth Edition of the First Volume of the History of the Pyrates, etc." It was thought by some people that the second volume was issued with the Second Edition, and some copies have been found bound up as if this were so; it is obvious from the above that this is a mistaken idea.

Octavo. The present copy measures $7\frac{7}{8}$ ins. by $4\frac{7}{8}$ ins.; that in the Henry E. Huntington Library, California, $7\frac{1}{2}$ ins. by $4\frac{1}{2}$ ins.

On p. 335 is a letter to the author, signed J. Evans, with the date Feb. 2, 1727-8.

1726.

8. HISTOIRE / DES PIRATES / ANGLOIS / Depuis leur Etablissement dans l'Isle de / la Providence, jusq' a present, / Contenant toutes leurs Avantures, Pirateries, / Meurtes, Cruautez & Exces / Avec / La vie et les Avantures / Des deux Femmes Pirates / Marie Read & Anne Bonney / Et un Extrait des Loix & des Ordonnances / concernant la Piraterie / Traduite de l'Anglois / Du Capitaine Charles Johnson. / Second Edition corrigee / (*ornament*) / A Paris. / Chez Etienne Ganeau, rue S. Jacques, / aux Armes de Dombes, pres de la rue Platre. / Et / Guillaume Cavelier Fils, rue Saint / Jacques, au Lys d'Or / M. DCC. XXVI / Avec Approbation & Privilege du Roy. /

Octavo. Mr. F. S. Parks' (of Massachusetts) copy measures 6½ ins. by 3¾ ins.

Signatures.—A to Hh (5 leaves) in eights and fours.

Pagination.—Title, introduction pp. i to lvi, pp. 1 to 365. At the end is a list of books published by Messrs. Ganeau and Cavelier fils.

Collation supplied by Mr. Parks.

Published as a fourth volume appendix to Esquemeling's " Histoire des Aventuriers, Filibustiers," etc.

1734.

9. A GENERAL / HISTORY / OF THE / LIVES AND AD-
VENTURES / OF THE MOST FAMOUS / HIGHWAY-
MEN, MURDERERS, STREET-ROBBERS, ETC. /
To which is added, / A Genuine Account of the Voyages and
Plunders / of the most Notorious Pyrates. / (*rule*) / Inter-
spersed with several diverting Tales, and pleasant Songs. /
(*rule*) / And Adorned with the Heads of the most Remarkable
Villains, Curiously / Engraven on Copper. / (*rule*) / By
Captain Charles Johnson. / (*rule*) / —Little Villains oft'
submit to Fate, / That Great Ones may enjoy the World in
State.   Garth. / (*rule*) / (*ornament*) / (*double rule*) / London:
/ Printed for and Sold by J. Janeway, in White-Fryers; and
by the Booksellers / of London and Westminster. / (*short
rule*) / MDCCXXXIV. /

Folio.   The present copy, one in the finest condition,
measures 14⅝ ins. by 9½ ins.

Signatures.—(A) (1 leaf-title), B to 6K in twos.

Pagination.—Title, verso blank, introduction pp. (1.) and
(2.), pp. (3) to 484, index pp. (485) and (486).   There are a
frontispiece and 25 engraved plates, by J. Basire after Nicholl
and others, facing pp. 20, 32, 89, 92, 106, 120, 132, 136, 163,
188, 189, 197, 203, 214, 228, 262, 267, 278, 307, 335, 372,
461, 466, 472, 483.

P. 4 is misnumbered 8, pp. 177 to 184 are misnumbered
187 to 194; pp. 324 and 325 reads 326 and 327; p. 379 reads
382, and 382 reads 379; and p. 410 reads 406.

Printed in double columns, the title in red and black, and
adorned with many beautiful head and tail pieces.

9a. The following advertisement appeared in the *Gentleman's Magazine*, June, 1734:

Just published, *The 14th Monthly Number.*

(*Adorned with two Curious Copper Plates of ' Squire* Thynn *murder'd, and the* Golden Farmer *robbing a Tinker.*')

The Lives and adventures of the most famous Highwaymen, Murderers, Pyrates, etc. By Capt. Charles Johnson. Two sheets of this work is publish'd every week for twopence; and Eight Sheets will be every Month stitch'd in Blue Paper for those who don't chuse to be troubled with weekly Subscriptions, at the Price of Eight Pence, except when Cuts, which will be only one Half-penny more; and the whole will be adorn'd with Prints of the most remarkable stories, curiously Engraved on Copper.

Printed for J. Janeway, at the Golden-Ball in White-Friars; and Sold by the Booksellers in Town and Country.

Note. If any of our Subscribers are neglected, and will please to send to J. Janeway *by the* Penny-Post, *the* Postage *shall be allowed, and particular Care shall be taken for the Future.*

1736.

10. A GENERAL / HISTORY / OF THE / LIVES AND AD-
VENTURES / OF THE MOST FAMOUS / HIGH-
WAYMEN, MURDERERS, STREET-ROBBERS, &C. /
From the Famous / Sir John Falstaff in the Reign of K.
Henry IV, 1399 to 1733. / To which is added, / A Genuine
Account of the Voyages and Plunders / of the most Notorious
Pyrates. / Interspersed with diverting Tales, and Pleasant
Songs. / And Adorned with Six and Twenty Large Copper
Plates, Engraved by the best Masters. / By Capt. Charles
Johnson. / . . . / London: / Printed for and Sold by Olive
Payne, at Horace's-Head, in Round-Court / in the Strand;
over-against York-Buildings. / M.DCC.XXXVI. /

Folio.   The Henry E. Huntington Library, California,
copy measures 14¼ ins. by 9¼ ins.

Signatures.—A to 6K in twos.   One leaf without signature
mark.

Pagination.—Title, verso blank, introduction 2 pp., pp. 3
to 484, index pp. 485-86.   There are a frontispiece and
plates.   The title is printed in red and black.

Collation supplied by the Henry E. Huntington Library.

1741.

11. A COMPLEAT / HISTORY / OF THE / LIVES AND
EXTRAORDINARY ADVENTURES / OF THE MOST
FAMOUS / PYRATES, HIGHWAYMEN, MURDERERS,
/ STREET-ROBBERS, ETC. / Also, a Genuine Account
of the / Voyages, Travels, and Plunders, / Of each particular
Hero, with an exact Description / of every Engagement,
Robbery, Murder, etc. / (*rule*) / Sir Richard Steele, in his
Englishman, No. 48, after an Introductory / Discourse on
Ambition, which he considers as the Motive of all / rapacious
and inhuman Actions, speaks of a Work of this Nature as / of
a curious Piece, and adds, That there is a Satisfaction to
Curiosity, / in knowing the Adventures of the meanest of
Mankind . . . and that / he had more Respect for these
Great Men in their Way, than for greater / Criminals, who
are described with Praise by more eminent Writers: / For
which he gives this Reason, That Du Vall, and others (whose
Lives / are contain'd in this Work) discover'd in many of
their Actions, that / they had a remaining Sense of Honour. /
(*rule*) / Felix quem faciunt aliena pericula cautum. / (*rule*) /
Salisbury, / Printed by and for Benjamin Collins, Bookseller
at the / Bible and Crown, in Silver-Street, / (*short rule*) /
MDCCXLI. /

Folio. The present copy, kindly lent for collation by
Mr. W. T. Spencer, is uncut and measures $12\frac{1}{4}$ ins. by $7\frac{1}{4}$ ins.
—it is unfortunately lacking several leaves at the end, so a full
record of signature and pagination cannot be given.

Signatures.—Starting at B on the first page of the introduction, repeating B and continuing in twos.

Pagination.—Title, verso blank, introduction pp. (1) and
(2), p. 3 to . . .

Printed in double columns with the title-page in black
and red.

1742.

12. A GENERAL AND TRUE / HISTORY / OF THE /
LIVES AND ACTIONS / OF THE MOST FAMOUS/
HIGHWAYMEN, MURDERERS, STREET-ROBBERS,
ETC. / To which is added, / A Genuine Account of the
Voyages and Plunders / of the most Noted Pirates. / Inter-
spersed with several Remarkable / Tryals / Of the most /
Notorious Malefactors, / at the / Sessions-House in the
Old Baily, London. / (*rule*) / Adorn'd with the Effigies, and
other material Transactions of the most / remarkable Offen-
ders, engraved on Copper-Plates. / (*rule*) / By Capt. Charles
Johnson. / (*rule*) / —Little Villains oft' submit to Fate, /
That Great Ones may enjoy the World in State.   Garth. /
(*rule*) / Birmingham: / Printed by R. Walker, at the Sign
of the Printing-Press, over- / against the Swan-Tavern in
the High-Street. / (*rule*) / MDCCXLII. /

Folio.   The present copy measures 11½ ins. by 7⅛ ins.

Signatures.—(A) to 5Q in twos.

Pagination.—Title, verso blank, introduction 2 pp (unnumbered), pp. 1 to 427, index pp. 427 and (428).   There
are an engraved frontispiece and 16 engraved plates facing
pp. 29, 31, 50, 79, 95, 121, 126, 143, 150, 155, 180, 218, 220,
281, 312, and 349, by H. Burgh, B. Cole, etc.

Pages 122 and 123 are misnumbered 121 and 122, p. 233
reads 230, 236 reads 233, and 336 reads 332.

Printed in double columns with the title in black and red.

1744.

13. HISTOIRE / DES / PIRATES / ANGLOIS. Depuis leur
Etablissement dans l'Isle / de la Providence jusqu'a présent. /
Contenant toutes leurs Avantures, Pirateries, / Meurtres,
Cruautés, Excès, &c. / Avec / La Vie Et Les Avantures /
De deux Femmes Pirates / Marie Read / & Anne Bonny. /
Et un Extrait des Loix & des Ordonnances / concernant la
Piraterie. / Traduite de l'Anglois. / Du Capitaine Charles
Johnson / Quatrieme Tome. / (*ornament*) / A Trevoux /
Par la Compagnie / (*double rule*) / M. DCC. XLIV. /

Duodecimo.   The present copy measures 6⅝ ins. by 3⅞ ins.
Mr. F. S. Parks' (of Massachusetts) copy measures 6½ ins.
by 3⅞ ins.

Signatures.—A and C in twelves, i (6 leaves), A to O in
twelves, P (eleven leaves).

Pagination.—Title, verso blank, introduction pp. (i) to lx,
pp. 1 to (358).   There are no illustrations.

This edition is the fourth volume, and appendix, of a
French translation of Esquemeling's "Buccaneers of
America."

1753.

14. A / GENERAL HISTORY / OF THE / LIVES AND AD-
VENTURES / OF THE / MOST FAMOUS HIGHWAY-
MEN, MURDERERS, / STREET-ROBBERS, AND
PYRATES. / The Whole interspersed with several divert- /
ing Tales, and Embellished with the / Heads of the most
remarkable Villains, / neatly Engraved. / (*rule*) / By Capt.
Mackelcan. / (*rule*) / Little Villains oft submit to Fate, /
That Great Ones may enjoy the World in State.   Garth. /
(*double rule*) / London: / Printed for R. Richards, the Corner
/ of Bernard's-Inn, in Holborn. / (*short rule*) / MDCCLIII. /

Octavo.   The present copy measures 7 ins. by 4¼ ins.

Signatures.—(A) (7 leaves), B to Ss in fours.

Pagination.—Title, verso blank, introduction pp. III to VI,
list of contents pp. VII to VIII, pp. 3 to 47, p. (48) blank,
3 to 52, 3 to 324.   There are an engraved frontispiece of
Robin Hood and William Stukely and 8 engraved plates,
by B. Cole, facing pp. 3 (second occurrence), 3 (third occurrence), 37, 84, 107, 157, 225, and 229.

The second occurrence of p. 11 is unnumbered.

The book is an abridged Johnson, and was probably published in three parts.

1758.

15. A GENERAL / HISTORY / OF THE / LIVES AND ADVENTURES / OF THE MOST FAMOUS /

Highwaymen,	Street-Robbers,
Murderers,	and
Pirates,	Thief-Takers,

Particularly / The four last most noted Villains, viz. / Macdaniel, Salmon, / Eagan and Berry. / As also of that notorious Accomplice of theirs, / Mary Jones and Others. / Shewing / The diabolical Arts by them practised, to get innocent / Persons convicted for Robberies, and to share amongst / themselves the Rewards paid for such Convictions. / The Whole / Interspersed with several diverting Tales, embellished / with the Heads of the most remarkable Villains, neatly / Engraved. / (*rule*) / By Capt. Mackdonald / (*double rule*) / London: / Printed for J. Warcus's, at the Indian Queen in the / Poultry, and H. Serjeant at the Star without Temple / Bar. M.DCCLVIII. /

Octavo. The present copy measures 6⅞ ins. by 4¼ ins.

Signatures.—(A) (1 leaf-title), B to Eee in fours, Fff (3 leaves).

Pagination.—Title, verso blank, pp. (1) to 418. There are an engraved frontispiece and 11 engraved plates, mostly by B. Cole, facing pp. 7, 50, 98, 129, 163, 183, 231, 297, 301, 337, 353.

Pp. 337 and 338 are missed in the numbering of the pages. See No. 14.

1772.

16. THE / HISTORY / OF THE / LIVES / AND / EXTRA-
ORDINARY ADVENTURES / OF THE MOST FAMOUS
/ PYRATES, HIGHWAYMEN, MURDERERS, /
STREET-ROBBERS, ETC. / Also a Genuine Account of
the / Voyages, Travels, and Plunders of each particu- / lar
Hero, with an exact description of every En- / gagement,
Robbery, Murder, etc. / (*double rule*) / (*ornament*) / (*double
rule*) / Portsmouth: / Printed and sold by R. Carr, Corner of
the Grand Parade, / (*short rule*) / MDCCLXXII. /

Octavo.   The present copy measures $8\frac{1}{4}$ ins. by $5\frac{1}{8}$ ins.

Signatures.—(A) to LII in fours, Mmm (2 leaves).

Pagination.—Title, verso blank, introduction pp. (3) and
(4), pp. (5) to 460.   There is a frontispiece portrait of Captain
Misson which is a bad copy of that of Captain Bartholomew
Roberts in the folio of 1534.

Page 83 is numbered 84 and *vice versa*, and the number in
each case is printed on the inside of the page.

The "Lives" of the pirates are taken from Johnson.

1774.

17. HISTOIRE / DES / PIRATES / ANGLOIS / Depuis leur Etablissement dans l'Isle de / la Providence jusqu'à présent. / Contenant toutes leurs Aventures, Pirateries, / Meurtres, Cruautés, Excès, etc. / Avec / La Vie et Les Aventures / De deux Femmes Pirates, / Marie Read et Anne Bonny, / Et un Extrait des Loix et des ordonnances / concernant la Piraterie. / Traduite de l'Anglois, / Du Capitaine Charles Johnson, Quatrieme Tome. / (*ornament*) / A Lyon, / Chez Benoît et Joseph Duplain, / Pere & Fils. / (*double rule*) / M.DCC.LXXIV. / Avec Privilege du Roi. /

Duodecimo. The present copy measures $6\frac{3}{8}$ ins. by $3\frac{5}{8}$ ins.

Signatures.—a to c in sixes, A to O in twelves, P (11 leaves).

Pagination.—Title, verso blank, introduction pp. (i) to lx. pp. (1) to 356, list of contents pp. (357) and (358).

This edition is the fourth volume, and appendix, of a French translation of Esquemeling's " Buccaneers of America."

1775.

18. HISTOIRE / DES / PIRATES / ANGLOIS / Depuis
leur Etablissement dans l'Isle de / la Providence jusqu'à
présent. / Contenant toutes leurs Aventures, Pirateries, /
Meurtres, Cruautés, Excès, etc. / Avec / La Vie et Les
Aventures / De deux Femmes Pirates, / Marie Read et
Anne Bonny, / Et un Extrait des Loix et des ordonnances /
concernant la Piraterie. / Le tout enrichi de Cartes Géo-
graphiques et de Figures en tailledouce. / Traduite de
l'Anglois, / Du Capitaine Charles Jonhson, / Tome
Quatrieme. / (*ornament*) / A Trevoux, / Par la Compagnie. /
(*ornamental rule*) / M.DCC.LXXV. /

Duodecimo.   The London Library copy measures 6½ ins.
by 3⅞ ins.; that of Mr. F. S. Parks (of Massachusetts), 6⅝ ins.
by 3¹¹⁄₁₆ ins.

Signatures.—a to c in sixes, A to O in twelves, P (11
leaves).

Pagination.—Title, verso blank, introduction pp. (i) to lx,
pp. (1) to 355, list of contents pp. (356) and (357), p. (358)
blank.

This edition is the fourth volume, and appendix, of a
French translation of Esquemeling's "Buccaneers of
America."   Contrary to the statement on the title-page, it
has no illustrations or maps.

1801.

19. LIVES / OF / MOST REMARKABLE / FEMALE
ROBBERS. / (*double rule*) / The German Princess, a Robber
& Imposter. / Moll Cut-purse, a Pickpocket & Highway-
woman. /

> Mary Read, } Pirates. /
> Anne Bonny, }

Nan Hereford, a Cheat & Imposter. / (*rule*) / Written by
Captain C. Johnson, / Author of Lives of the Highwaymen,
&c. / (*long double rule*) / London: Printed by T. Maiden,
Sherbourne-Lane, / For Ann Lemoine, White-Rose Court,
Coleman- / Street, and Sold by T. Hurst, / Paternoster
Row. / (*short rule*) / 1801. / [Price Six-Pence.] /

Duodecimo.   The British Museum copy measures 6⅞ ins
by 4 ins.

Signatures.—A to C in sixes, D (5 leaves).

Pagination.—Title, verso blank, pp. (3) to 48.   There is an
engraved frontispiece.

1813.

20. THE / HISTORY / OF THE / LIVES AND ACTIONS /
OF THE MOST FAMOUS / HIGHWAYMEN, STREET-
ROBBERS, / ETC. ETC. / To which is added, a genuine
Account of / the Voyages and Plunders / of the most noted /
Pirates. / (*short double rule*) / By Captain Charles Johnson. /
(*short double rule*) / " . . . Little Villains oft' submit to fate,
/ " That great ones may enjoy the world in state." Garth. /
(*short double rule*) / Edinburgh: / Printed by John Moir,
Royal Bank Close, / for Longman, Hurst, Rees, Orme, &
Brown, / London. / 1813. /

Octavo. The present copy is an uncut one measuring
9 ins. by 5½ ins.

Signatures.—A to Kk in eights, Ll (2 leaves).

Pagination.—Title, verso blank, advertisement p. (iii)
p. (iv) blank, list of contents pp. (v) to viii, pp. (9) to 539,
p. (540) blank, blank leaf. There is an engraved frontispiece.

The present copy has 12 pp. of advertisements inserted
at the end.

1814.

21. THE / HISTORY / OF THE / LIVES AND ACTIONS / OF THE MOST FAMOUS / HIGHWAYMEN, STREET-ROBBERS, / ETC. ETC. ETC. / To which is added, / a genuine account of the / Voyages and Plunders / of the most noted / Pirates. / By Captain Charles Johnson. / (*short double rule*) / A New Edition. / (*short double rule*) / " —Little Villains oft' submit to fate, / " That great ones may enjoy the world in state." Garth. / (*short double rule*) / Edinburgh; / Printed for John Thomson Jun. and Co. Edinburgh; / Longman, Hurst, Rees, Orme, and Brown, London: / and John Cumming, Dublin. / 1814. /

Octavo. The present copy measures $8\frac{3}{4}$ ins. by $5\frac{1}{2}$ ins.

Signatures.—(A) (4 leaves) B to 2N in eights, 2O (3 leaves).

Pagination.—Title, verso blank, advertisement p. (iii), p. (iv) blank, list of contents pp. (v) to viii, pp. (9) to 574.

In the present copy there are 8 pp. of advertisements inserted at the front of the volume, and dated May, 1816.

1814.

22. THE / HISTORY / OF / THE PIRATES, / containing / The Lives / of / those noted pirate Captains, / Misson, Bowen, Kidd, Tew, Halsey, White, / Condent, Bellamy, Fly, Howard, / Lewis, Cornelius, Williams, / Burgess, North, / And Their Several Crews. / Also, an Account of the Piracies and Cruelties of / John Augur, William Cunningham, Dennis Mac- / karthy, William Dowling, William Lewis, Tho- / mas Morris, George Bendall, and William Ling, / who were tried, condemned and executed at / Nassau, New-Providence, on Friday, the 12th of / October, 1718. To which is added, / A Description of Magadoxa, / in Ethiopia. / (*ornament*) / By Capt. Charles Johnson. / (*ornament*) / Omne tulit punctum, qui miscuit utile dulci. Hor. / (*rule*) / London, Printed. / Norwich: Re-printed by R. Hubbard. / 1814. /

Duodecimo. The British Museum copy measures $6\frac{1}{2}$ ins. by $3\frac{3}{4}$ ins.; the Boston Public Library copy, $6\frac{1}{4}$ ins. by $3\frac{1}{2}$ ins.; Mr. F. S. Parks' (of Massachusetts) copy, $6\frac{3}{8}$ ins. by $3\frac{3}{4}$ ins.

Signatures.—A (5 leaves), B to Z in sixes.

Pagination.—Title, verso blank, pp. 3 to 288. No illustrations.

An abridged edition of Vol. II. of Johnson's " History."

1822.

23. LIVES / AND / ADVENTURES / OF THE MOST CELE-
BRATED / HIGHWAYMEN, / STREET-ROBBERS,
ETC. / By / Capt. Jas. Johnson. / —Little Villains oft
submit to fate, / That great ones may enjoy the World in
state. / London / Pubd. by Hodgson & Co. 43, King St.
Snow Hill & 43, Holywell St. / Strand.

Octavo.   The present copy, an uncut one, measures $8\frac{3}{4}$ ins.
by $5\frac{1}{2}$ ins.

Signatures.—1B to 3I in fours, 3K and 4L (2 leaves), 4M
and 4N in fours, 5O (2 leaves), 5P and 5Q in fours, 6R (2
leaves), 6S to 7X in fours, 7Y (2 leaves), 8Z and 8^2A in fours,
8^2B (2 leaves), 9^2C (4 leaves), 9^2D (2 leaves), 9^2E and
10^2F in fours, 10^2G (2 leaves), 10^2H to 11^2K in fours, 11^2L
(2 leaves), 12^2M and 12^2N in fours, 12^2O (2 leaves), 13^2P and
13^2Q in fours, 13^2R (2 leaves), 14^2S and 14^2T in fours, 14^2U
(2 leaves).

Pagination.—Title, verso blank, pp. (1) to 286, index pp.
(287) and (288).   There are a coloured frontispiece and 8
coloured plates facing pp. 67, 77, 89, 155, 179, 240, 264, 273.

The engraved title is within an etched border, and is from
a drawing by G. Cruikshank.   None of the plates are by
Cruikshank.   There is no printed title.

The volume is undated, but the plate facing p. 264 bears
the date Aug. 2, 1822.

This is the Second Edition.   The first was under the
imprint of C. Smeeton, St. Martin's Churchyard, Charing
Cross.

1825.

24. THE / HISTORY / OF / THE PIRATES / containing / The
Lives / of / Those Noted Pirate Captains / Misson, Bowen,
Kidd, Tew, Halsey, White, Con / dent, Bellamy, Fly,
Howard, Lewis, Cor / nelius, Williams, Burgess, North, /
And their several Crews. / Also, an Account of the Piracies
and Cruelties / of John Augur, William Cunningham, Dennis
Mac- / karthy, William Dowling, William Lewis, Thomas /
Morris, George Bendall, / and William Ling, who / were
tried, condemned and executed at Nassau, / New Providence,
on the 12th of October, 1718. / To which is added, / A
Correct Account of the / Late Piracies / committed in the
West Indies; / and the / Expedition of Com. Porter. /
(*double rule*) / Omne tulit punctum, qui miscuit utile dulci.
—Hor. / Haverhill, Mass. / Published by Thomas Carey, /
1825. /

Duodecimo. The Boston Public Library copy and that
of Mr. F. S. Parks (of Massachusetts) both measure $6\frac{7}{8}$ ins.
by $4\frac{1}{8}$ ins.

Signatures.—1 to 23 in sixes.

Pagination.—Title, pp. 1 to 276. Pp. 1 to 245 is Johnson's
" History." On verso of title is a paragraph signed by
the clerk of the District Court of Massachusetts giving
Thomas Carey the proprietary rights of the book. There is
a frontispiece.

1825?.

25. JOHNSON'S LIVES OF HIGHWAYMEN, &C. / (*double rule*) / Sawney Beane; / or, / The Highland / Murderer and Man-Eater: / (*long double rule*) / Together with / The Lives / of the / Golden Farmer, / Dick Walton, the Conjurer, / and / Tom Gerrard, / an / incorrigible incendiary & housebreaker. / By Captain Charles Johnson. / " What monstrous Days are these ? / Not only to be vicious most Men study / But in it to be ugly, strive t'exceed / Each other in the most deformed Deed." / (*long double rule*) / London: / Printed and Published by J. Lee, / 24, Half-Moon-Street, near Sun-Street, Bishopsgate; / Sold by J. Bysh, Paternoster-Row, and by the Booksellers. / (*rule*) / Six-Pence. /

Duodecimo. The British Museum copy measures 7 ins. by $4\frac{1}{8}$ ins.

Signatures.—B (6 leaves), C (7 leaves).

Pagination.—Title, verso blank, pp. (1) to (26) unpaged. There is a coloured frontispiece. The pamphlet has blue paper covers. Another title, differing in the wording and arrangement from the title-page, is printed on the front cover.

The date of publication is about 1825.

1827.

26. THE / HISTORY / OF / THE PIRATES, / containing / The Lives / of / Those Noted Pirate Captains, / Misson, Bowen, Kidd, Tew, Halsey, White, Condent, / Bellamy, Fly, Howard, Lewis, Cornelius, / Williams, Burgess, North, / And Their Several Crews. / Also, / An Account Of The Piracies And Cruelties / Of / John Augur, William Cunningham, Dennis Mackarthy, / William Dowling, William Lewis, Thomas Morris, / George Bendall, and William Ling, / Who Were Tried, Condemned, and Executed / at Nassau, New Providence, / On The / Tenth of December, 1718. / To which is added, / A Correct Account Of The / Late Piracies / Committed In The West Indies; / And the / Expedition Of Commodore Porter / (*rule*) / Omne tulit punctum, qui miscuit utile dulci.—Hor. / (*double rule*) / Stereotyped By James Conner, New York. / Published By Henry Benton / 1827. /

Duodecimo.   The Henry E. Huntington Library (California) copy measures 6¾ ins. by 4¼ ins.

Signatures.—1 to 23 in sixes, 24 (four leaves.)

Pagination.—Title, verso bearing copyright notice for the District of Massachusetts, pp. (5) to 283.   There is a frontispiece.   Page 239 is wrongly numbered 139.

1828.

27. SPECIMENS / OF THE / YORKSHIRE DIALECT, / by way of dialogue, / containing / A Dialogue / between / Gulwell, a London Register Office Keeper / and / Margery Moorpoot, a country girl, / Auld Daisy, An Eclogue, / A cock and bull story, / The Hireing, The Bellman of Ripon, / The Yorkshire Tyke, &c, / To which is added / A copious glossary, / and the / Life of William Nevinson. / (*double rule*) / London: Orlando Hodgson, / Maiden Lane, Cheapside. / (*short rule*) / 1828. /

Duodecimo.—The British Museum copy measures $6\frac{15}{16}$ ins. by 4 ins.

No signatures.

Pagination.—Title, verso blank, pp. (3) to 24. P. (17) has half-title, The Life of William Nevinson, Written by Captain Johnson. The "Life" is not in the Yorkshire dialect.

1829.

28. THE / HISTORY / OF / THE PIRATES, / containing / the
Lives / of / those noted Pirate Captains, / Misson, Bowen,
Kidd, Tew, Halsey, White, Condent, / Bellamy, Fly, Howard,
Lewis, Cornelius, / Williams, Burgess, North, / and their
several crews. / Also, / an Account of the Piracies and
Cruelties / of / John Augur, William Cunningham,
Dennis Mackarthy, / William Dowling, William Lewis,
Thomas Morris, / George Bendall, and William Ling, /
who were tried, condemned, and executed / on the / Tenth
of December, 1718. / To which is added, / a correct account
of the / Late Piracies / committed in the West Indies; / and
the / Expedition of Commodore Porter. / (*short rule*) / Omne
tulit punctum, qui miscuit utile dulci.—Hor. / Hartford: /
Published by Henry Benton. / (*short rule*) / 1829. /

Duodecimo.   The present copy measures 6¾ ins. by 4⅛ ins.

Signatures.—(1) to 23 in sixes, 24 (4 leaves).

Pagination.—Title, verso blank, p. (3) copyright certificate
of the District of Massachusetts, p. (4) blank, pp. (5) to 283,
p. (284) blank.   Pp. (5) to 216 is a reprint of Vol. II. of
Johnson's "History of the Pyrates."   There is a woodcut
frontispiece.

(*Circa*) **1830.**

29. THE / HISTORY AND LIVES / OF THE MOST / NO-
TORIOUS / PIRATES, / AND / THEIR CREWS: /
narrating a series of / Gallant Sea Fights, / Daring Attacks,
Sanguinary Murders, / Horrid Cruelties, and Barbarities. /
(*rule*) / Describing their debauched and profligate / manner of
Living; their / Laws, Customs, Places of Refuge, / etc. etc. /
(*rule*) / By an old Seaman. / (*rule*) / Embellished with Plates.
/ (*rule*) / London: / J. Duncombe, 19 Little Queen Street,
/ Holborn. /

16mo. The present copy measures 4 ins. by 2½ ins.

Signatures.—(B) to Q in sixteens, R (10 leaves).

Pagination.—Title, verso blank, half-title: The / Miniature
Library: / Volume the first. / (*small woodcut*) / (*rule*) / With
engravings / (*rule*) / London. / J. Duncombe, Queen Street,
Holborn. /, preface 2 pp., list of contents pp. (1) and (2),
pp. (3) to 250. There is a frontispiece and 6 plates.

Vol. II. is prefaced by a reproduction of the above half-
title, " Volume the first " having substituted for it " Volume
the second," and proceeds straight on with the text. There
are no plates to the present copy of Vol. II.

This book was printed as one of the titles in a series. It is
taken mainly from Johnson, but does not reproduce him
wholly or his exact wording in all places, as many of the other
unacknowledged editions do. The date of publication is
somewhere about 1830.

1834.

30. LIVES AND EXPLOITS / OF / ENGLISH HIGHWAY-
MEN, / PIRATES AND ROBBERS, / drawn from the
earliest and most authentic / sources, and brought down to /
the present time. / By / C. Whitehead, Esq. / With sixteen
engravings by Messrs. Bagg. / In two volumes. / Vol. I (Vol.
II.) / London: / Bull and Churton, Holles Street. / 1834. /

Octavo.   The present copy measures 6½ ins. by 4 ins.

Vol. I.: Signatures.—b (4 leaves), B to Y in eights, Z
(6 leaves).

Pagination.—Engraved title, verso blank, title, verso
printer's name (Samuel Bentley) and address, preface pp.
(iii) to viii, list of contents pp. (ix) to xii, pp. (1) to 347,
p. (348) printer's name and address.   There are an engraved
frontispiece and 6 engraved plates facing pp. 68, 119, 197,
279, 297, and 335.   The engraved title is dated 1833.

Vol. II.: Signatures.—B to 2B in eights.

Pagination.—Title, verso printer's name and address, list
of contents pp. (iii) and iv, pp. (1) to 384.   There are
6 engraved plates facing pp. 25, 81, 105, 147, 228, and 313.

1834.

31. THE / HISTORY / OF / THE PIRATES / *etc.* *The title reads the same as the* Haverhill, 1825 *edition, substituting for* " Haverhill, etc.," Hartford / published by Henry Benton / 1834 /.

Duodecimo. Mr. F. S. Parks' (of Massachusetts) copy measures 6¾ ins. by 4½ ins.

Signatures.—1 to 23 in sixes, 24 (4 leaves).

Pagination.—Title, pp. 1 to (284). There is a frontispiece.

(*Circa*) 1834.

32. Another edition, the same as above except that " the Late Piracies " in the title is on one line instead of being divided " the / Late Piracies."

No date of publication.

1836.

33. LIVES OF THE MOST / NOTORIOUS HIGHWAYMEN / FOOTPADS AND MURDERERS. /

No signatures.

Pagination.—Pp. (1) to 288.

In 36 weekly numbers at one penny each, with an illustration on the first page of each number, from April 30th, 1836, to December 31st, 1836.

HISTORY OF THE PIRATES / OF / ALL NATIONS. /

No signatures.

Pagination.—Pp. (1) to 352.

In 44 weekly numbers at one penny each, with an illustration on the first page of each number, from March 5th, 1836, to December 31st, 1836.   Several numbers contain large extracts from Johnson.

Published by Lloyd, 44, Wych-Street; Purkess, Compton-Street, Soho; and Strange, Paternoster-Row (printed at the bottom of the last page of each number).

Octavo.   The present copy measures $8\frac{1}{4}$ ins. by $5\frac{1}{8}$ ins.

Printed in double columns.

1836.

34. THE / HISTORY / OF THE / LIVES AND BLOODY
EXPLOITS / OF THE / MOST NOTED / PIRATES; /
THEIR TRIALS AND EXECUTIONS. / Including A
Correct Account of The / Late Piracies / committed In The
West Indies, And The Expedition / Of Commodore Porter;
Also, Those committed / On The Brig Mexican, Who Were
Tried / And Executed At Boston, in 1835. / (*rule*) / " Omne
tulit punctum, qui miscuit utile dulci."—Hor. / (*rule*) /
Embellished With Engravings from Original Designs. /
(*cut showing* " The Ship Speaker Taken by Pirates.") /
Hartford, Ct.: / Published by Ezra Strong. / (*rule*) / 1836.

Duodecimo. Mr. F. S. Parks' (of Massachusetts) copy
measures 7⅜ ins. by 4½ ins.

Signatures.—1 to 24 in sixes, 25 (4 leaves).

Pagination.—Title, pp. 1 to 296. There are a frontispiece
and eight illustrations.

1839.

35. THE / LIVES AND ACTIONS / OF THE MOST NOTED / HIGHWAYMEN, / STREET-ROBBERS, PIRATES, / &C. &C. / By Captain Charles Johnson. / (*vignette*) / The third edition. / London: / Printed for Thomas Tegg, No. 73, Cheapside; / Tegg and Co., Dublin; / R. Griffin and Co., Glasgow; also J. and S. A. Tegg, Sydney and Hobart Town. / (*short rule*) / MDCCCXXXIX.

Duodecimo.   The present copy measures $8\frac{1}{2}$ ins. by 5 ins.

Signatures.—B to Y in twelves.

Pagination.—Title, verso blank, pp. (1) to 502; index pp. (503)-504.   There are an engraved frontispiece and 11 engraved plates facing pp. 41, 59, 80, 140, 295, 305, 344, 359, 367, 396, and 426.

This edition is a reprint of the 1813 Edinburgh edition, omitting the appendix.

Published in dark brown cloth, lettered in gilt on the back and bearing a blind stamp design on the sides.

1839.

36. THE / LIVES AND ACTIONS / OF THE MOST NOTED / HIGHWAYMEN, / STREET-ROBBERS, PIRATES, / &C. &C. / By Captain Charles Johnson. / (*vignette*) / The fourth edition. / London: / Printed for Thomas Tegg, No. 73, Cheapside; / Tegg and Co., Dublin; / R. Griffin and Co., Glasgow; / also, J. and S. A. Tegg, Sydney and Hobart Town. / (*short rule*) / MDCCCXXXIX. /

Duodecimo. The British Museum copy measures 7⅞ ins. by 4¾ ins.

Signatures.—B to Y in twelves.

Pagination.—Title, verso blank, pp. (1) to 502, index pp. (503)-504. There are an engraved frontispiece and 11 engraved plates facing pp. 41, 59, 81, 136, 294, 304, 344, 359, 367, 396 and 426. Following p. 504 is " A select catalogue of books (24 pp.) published by William Tegg & Co., London," which is dated 1847.

Published in red cloth, with gilt lettering on the back and bearing blind stamp design on sides.

1839.

37. THE / LIVES AND BLOODY EXPLOITS / OF THE / MOST NOTED / PIRATES, / THEIR TRIALS AND EXECUTIONS, / including correct accounts of the / Late Piracies, / committed in the West Indias and the Expedition / of Commodore Porter; also Those Committed / on the Brig Mexican, who were executed / At Boston, in 1835. / " Omne tulit punctum, qui miscuit utile dulci."—Hor. / (*vignette*) / Embellished with numerous plates from original designs. / (*double rule*) / Hartford, Con. / Published by Ezra Strong. / 1839. /

Duodecimo.   The Boston Public Library copy measures $7\frac{1}{2}$ ins. by $4\frac{1}{2}$ ins.   Mr. F. S. Parks' (of Massachusetts) copy measures $7\frac{1}{4}$ ins. by $4\frac{1}{4}$ ins.

Signatures.—1 to 24 in sixes, 25 (five leaves.)

Pagination.—Title, verso bearing copyright notice, pp. 1 to 298.

Note the spelling of Indias, and Connecticut with one n.

This was copyright 1837 by Ezra Strong, stereotyped by Shepard, Oliver and Co., Boston.   The plates seem to be the same as those of the Hartford 1855 edition, but the illustrations are differently arranged and have different captions. Johnson's " Lives, etc.," occupy pp. 1 to 252.

1842.

38. LIVES AND EXPLOITS / OF / ENGLISH HIGHWAY-
MEN, / PIRATES, & ROBBERS; / drawn from the
most authentic sources, / By Captain Charles Johnson. /
Revised & continued to the present time, / By C. Whitehead, Esq. / Embellished with Sixteen spirited Engravings. /
(*small engraving*) / " Little villains oft submit to fate, / That
great ones may enjoy the world in state." / London: / Henry
G. Bohn, York Street, Covent Garden. / MDCCCXLII. /

Octavo. The present copy measures 6¾ ins. by 4¼ ins.

Signatures.—B to Dd in eights, Ee (3 leaves).

Pagination.—Title, verso blank, preface pp. (v) to ix,
p. (x) blank, list of contents pp. (xi) and xii, pp (2) to 422.
There are 15 engraved plates facing pp. 2, 42, 67, 84, 168,
185, 190, 201, 223, 291, 303, 314, 331, 346, and 385.

Published in cloth decorated in gilt on back and front with
scenes illustrating the text.

1842.

39. LIVES AND EXPLOITS / OF / ENGLISH HIGHWAY-
MEN, / PIRATES, AND ROBBERS; / drawn from the
most authentic sources, / by / Capt. Charles Johnson. /
Revised and continued to the present time, / by / C.
Whitehead, Esq. / Embellished with sixteen spirited engrav-
ings. / —" Little villains oft submit to Fate, / That great
ones may enjoy the world in state." / London: / Henry G.
Bohn, York Street, Covent Garden. / MDCCXLII. /

Duodecimo. The present copy measures 6¾ ins. by 4¼ ins.

Signatures.—(A) to 2N in sixes, 2O (1 leaf).

Pagination.—Engraved title, verso blank, title, verso blank,
preface pp. (v) to ix, p. (x) blank, list of contents pp. (xi)
and xii, half-title, verso blank, pp. 1 to 422. There are an
engraved frontispiece, an engraved vignette on the engraved
title-page, and 14 engraved plates facing pp. 42, 67, 84, 168,
185, 190, 201, 223, 291, 314, 303, 331, 346, 385.

Published in cloth ornamented on the back in gold and
on the sides in blind.

1844.

40. LIVES / OF / THE MOST NOTORIOUS AND DARING /
HIGHWAYMEN, / ROBBERS AND MURDERERS. /
Compiled from authentic sources, and brought / down to the
present time. / A New Edition. / Manchester: / Printed &
published by S. Johnson, & Son, / Livesey St., and Church
St., Liverpool. / (*short rule*) / 1844. /

32mo. The present copy measures 5 ins. by $3\frac{1}{8}$ ins.

Signatures.—(1) to 28 in eights.

Pagination.—Engraved title, verso blank, title, verso bears
the printer's name and address, list of contents p. (3), p. (4)
blank, pp. (5) to 448. There are an engraved frontispiece
and an engraved title-page, which latter bears the imprint,
" Liverpool. Thomas Johnson, Dale Strt."

Published in cloth with a gilt back and blind stamped
sides.

1845.

41. LIVES AND EXPLOITS / OF THE MOST / CELE-
BRATED PIRATES / AND / SEA ROBBERS. / *(short
rule)* / By T. Douglas. / *(short rule)* / London: / Published
by J. S. Pratt. / *(short rule)* / MDCCCXLV.

32mo. The present copy measures 5 ins. by 3⅛ ins.

Signatures.—(A) to U in eights.

Pagination.—Half-title, verso blank, title, verso blank,
pp. (1) to 318, index pp. (319) and 320. There is a frontispiece coming between the half-title and the title.

Published in cloth with gilt lettering on the back and blind
stamped sides.

(*Circa*) 1850.

42. LIVES / OF / THE MOST NOTORIOUS AND DARING
/ HIGHWAYMEN, / ROBBERS AND MURDERERS. /
Compiled from authentic sources, and brought / down to the
present time. / A New Edition. / Liverpool: / Published by
Thomas Johnson, / Dale Street. /

This edition is a reissue of that of Manchester, 1844,
with a fresh title-page. It is bound in cloth bearing the
same design.

(*Circa*) **1850.**

43. THE / LIVES AND ADVENTURES / OF THE MOST
NOTED / HIGHWAYMEN, PIRATES, / HOUSE-
BREAKERS, STREET ROBBERS, / ETC. ETC. / By
Captain Charles Johnson. / (*vignette*) / London: / David
Bryce, Paternoster Row, / and all booksellers. /

Octavo. The present copy measures 6⅞ ins. by 4⅜ ins.

Signatures.—(1) to 31 in eights, 32 (6 leaves).

Pagination.—Title, verso bears printer's (Savill and
Edwards) name and address, introductory remarks 2 pp., pp.
(1) to 504. There are an engraved frontispiece and 11
engraved plates facing pp. 45, 59, 84, 141, 184, 296, 334, 359,
367, 397 and 426.

Published in cloth bearing on the back and front cover
illustrations, in gilt, of the subject of the book. This collation
was made from two copies, one bound in red cloth and the
other in blue.

1850.

44. THE / LIVES AND EXPLOITS / OF THE MOST / NOTORIOUS PIRATES / AND / THEIR CREWS. / (*short rule*) / By a Sea Captain. / (*short rule*) / Halifax: / Printed and published by William Milner, / Cheapside. / (*short rule*) / MDCCL. /

32mo.   The present copy measures 5 ins. by $3\frac{1}{8}$ ins.

Signatures.—None.

Pagination.—Engraved title, verso blank, title, verso blank, pp. (7) to 322, list of contents pp. (323) and 324. There is an engraved frontispiece, the engraved title-page bears a vignette illustration, but no imprint or date.

Published in cloth with the back ornamented in gilt, and a gilt design of a ship on the front cover.

1855.

45. THE / HISTORY / OF THE / LIVES AND BLOODY EXPLOITS / OF THE / MOST NOTED / PIRATES; / THEIR / TRIALS AND EXECUTIONS. / Including a correct account of the / Late Piracies / committed in the West Indies, and the Expedition / of Commodore Porter; also, those committed / on the Brig Mexican, who were tried / and executed at Boston in 1835. / (*rule*) / " Omne tulit punctum, qui miscuit utile dulci "—Hor. / (*rule*) / Embellished with Engravings from Original Designs. / (*vignette*) / The Ship Speaker taken by the Pirates,—Page 112. / Hartford: / Published by Silas Andrus & Son. / 1855. /

Duodecimo. The Boston Public Library copy measures 7 ins. by 4¼ ins.

Signatures.—1 to 12 in twelves, 13 (five leaves).

Pagination.—Title, verso bearing copyright notice, pp. 1 to 298. There are eight illustrations.

This edition was copyright 1836 by Ezra Strong. Stereotyped by Shepard, Oliver and Co., Boston. Johnson's " History of the Lives, etc," occupies pp. 1 to 252.

1856.

46. LIVES, / EXPLOITS, AND CRUELTIES / OF / THE MOST CELEBRATED / PIRATES / AND / SEA ROBBERS. / Brought down to the latest period. / Halifax: / Milner and Sowerby. / (*short rule*) / 1856. /

32mo.   The present copy measures 5 ins. by $3\frac{1}{4}$ ins.

Signatures.—(A) to 2E in eights.

Pagination.—Engraved title, verso blank, title, verso blank, list of pirates p. (3), p. (4) blank, pp. (5) to 448.   There is an engraved frontispiece and a vignette illustration on the engraved title-page.

Published in cloth with gilt lettering on the back and the sides blind stamped.   The end papers of the present copy consist of advertisements headed Milner and Sowerby's Cheap List, the pages numbered 1 to 6.

1861.

47. Halifax.

Exactly similar to the above, except the date is 1861. The cloth cover is similar, but stamped with a different design.

1863.

48. LIVES / OF THE / MOST NOTORIOUS AND DARING / HIGHWAYMEN, / ROBBERS, AND MURDERERS. / Compiled from authentic sources, / and brought down to a recent period. / A New Edition. / Halifax: / Milner and Sowerby. / (*short rule*) / 1863. /

32mo. The present copy measures 5 ins. by $3\frac{1}{4}$ ins.

Signatures.—None.

Pagination.—Engraved title, verso blank, title, verso blank, list of contents p. (3), p. (4) blank, pp. (5) to 448. There is an engraved frontispiece and a vignette illustration on the engraved title-page.

In the same style of binding and having the end-paper advertisements as in the Halifax edition of 1856. The back of this copy bears, in addition to the title and in blind lettering, " The Cottage Library."

(*Circa*) **1870.**

49. LIVES AND EXPLOITS / OF THE / MOST NOTORIOUS
    AND DARING / HIGHWAYMEN, / ROBBERS, MUR-
    DERERS, / FORGERS, AND TRAITORS. / Compiled
    from authentic sources, / and brought down to modern
    times. / (*ornamental rule*) / Wakefield: / William Nicholson
    and Sons. / London: S. D. Ewins & Co., Paternoster Row. /
    (*small ornament*). /

Octavo.   The present copy measures $5\frac{5}{8}$ ins. by $3\frac{3}{4}$ ins.

Signatures.—(A) to Z in eights.

Pagination.—Half-title, verso blank, title, verso blank,
pp. (5) to 413, p. (414) index.   There is a coloured mounted
frontispiece. Published in red cloth with lettering and
design in gilt and black on back and sides. It would
appear to have been published about 1870.

(*Circa*) 1870.

50. THE / LIVES AND EXPLOITS / OF THE MOST / NO-
TORIOUS PIRATES / AND / THEIR CREWS. / (*rule*) /
By a Sea Captain. / (*rule*) / London: / Richardson and Son,
172, Fleet St., / 9, Capel St. Dublin; and Derby. /

32mo.   The present copy measures 5 ins. by 3⅛ ins.

Signatures.—(1) to 20 in eights.

Pagination.—Engraved title, verso blank, title, verso
blank, pp. (7) to 322, p. (323) and 324 list of contents, with
the printer's name at the bottom of the last page.   There is
an engraved title and a vignette illustration of the engraved
title-page.

The engraved title bears the imprint, " Derby. Thomas
Richardson & Son."   This is, then, one of the copies bound
up for sale at the Derby establishment.

Published in cloth lettered in gilt on the back with a blind
stamp design on the sides.

(*Circa*) **1870.**

51. LIVES / OF / NOTORIOUS AND DARING / HIGHWAY-
MEN, ROBBERS, / AND / MURDERERS. / Compiled
from authentic sources. / (*rule*) / London: / Thomas Richardson and Son, / 26, Paternoster Row; 9, Capel Street, Dublin; /
and Derby. /

32mo. The present copy measures $5\frac{1}{8}$ ins. by $3\frac{1}{8}$ ins.

Signatures.—(1) to 20 in eights.

Pagination.—Engraved title, verso blank, title, verso
blank, pp. (7) to 324. There is an engraved frontispiece
and a vignette illustration on the engraved title-page.

The engraved title-page of this edition bears the imprint
Derby as the previous one does, but the two illustrations
are totally different and the list of contents does not occur
at the end of the book. It is obvious that it is an entirely
fresh printing.

Published in cloth lettered in gilt on the back, and bearing
a blind stamp design on the sides.

1883.

52. LIVES AND EXPLOITS / OF / ENGLISH HIGHWAY-MEN, / PIRATES, AND ROBBERS; / drawn from the most authentic sources, / By Capt. Charles Johnson, / With additions / By C. Whitehead, Esq. / Embellished with Twelve Spirited Engravings. / (*vignette*) / " Little villains oft submit to Fate, / That great ones may enjoy the World in State." / London: Printed for the Booksellers. / 1883. /

Octavo. The present copy measures 6¾ ins. by 4⅛ ins.

Signatures.—A (4 leaves), B to Dd in eights, Ee (3 leaves).

Pagination.—Title, verso blank, preface pp. (v) to x, contents pp. (xi) and xii, pp. (1) to 422. There is an engraved frontispiece and 10 engraved plates facing pp. 67, 168, 184, 192, 200, 224, 304, 312, 344 and 384.

Printer's name, Walter Scott, " Kenilworth Press." Felling and Newcastle, at the bottom of p. 422.

Published in cloth with illustrations in gilt on back and front cover.

1891.

53. (*vignette*) / THE BUCCANEERS / AND MAROONERS OF / AMERICA / (*vignette*) / Being an account of the / famous adventures and / daring deeds of certain / notorious freebooters / of the Spanish main / A new illustrated edition / Edited by Howard Pyle / London: T. Fisher Unwin, / Paternoster Square.   MDCCCXCI. /

Octavo.   The present copy measures 8 ins. by 5¼ ins.

Signatures.—1 to 25 in eights, 26 (two leaves).

Pagination.—Title, verso blank, list of contents pp. (5) to 11, p. (12) blank, list of illustrations p. 13, p. (14) blank, introduction pp. (15) to 41, p. (42) blank, pp. (43) to 403. The work is in two parts, Part I., pp. (43) to 236, containing part of the English translation of Esquemeling's " The History of the Buccaneers of America," and Part II., pp. (239) to 403, containing part of Captain Charles Johnson's " General History of the . . . Pyrates."   Page 237 has half-title, " A genuine account of four notorious / pirates."   The four are Captain Teach, Captain Kidd, Captain Roberts and Captain Avery.   P. (238) blank.   There is a frontispiece and 5 illustrations, those facing pp. 239 and 300 (Captains Teach and Roberts) being reproduced from second edition of Johnson.

Published in red cloth with gilt lettering on back and front cover.   The back and the front cover also bear in addition, " The Adventure Series " in black lettering.

1905.

54. Another edition of the above, but with "Popular edition" instead of "A new illustrated edition" on title-page, and dated 1905. It measures 7¾ ins. by 5 ins.

Signatures and pagination the same as 1891 edition.

Published in light blue cloth with white lettering on back and on front cover. The latter also bears designs of ships in dark blue.

Another issue of the Popular edition was published in light brown covers.

1908.

55. (*vignette*) / Captain Johnson / LIVES OF THE HIGHWAY-
MEN / with introduction by H. B. Marriott Watson /
(*vignette*) Sisley's Ltd. / Makers of Beautiful Books / London
/ (*vignette*) /

Octavo. The present copy measures 6¾ ins. by 4 ins.

Signatures.—A to T in eights.

Pagination.—Title, verso blank, introduction pp. iii to vi,
list of contents pp. vii-viii, pp. 1 to (304).

The book was published in 1908 and contains extracts
from 1734 edition.

[1913.]

56. PIRATES / With a Foreword and sundry Decorations by /
Lovat Fraser / (*cut*) / Published at Stationers' Hall Court in /
the County of London by / Simpkin Marshall Hamilton
Kent & Co / Ltᵈ / [1913]

Octavo. The present copy measures 8¼ ins. by 6¼ ins.

Signatures.—A to K in eights.

Pagination.—Title, verso blank, contents pp. v-vi,
foreword pp. vii to xvi, pp. (1) to 159, p. (160) blank.

There are a frontispiece and 7 illustrations.

The book is a reprint of the major part of the fifth (so-called)
edition of " The History and Lives of all the Most Notorious
Pirates, and their Crews," London, 1735. The latter is a
pirated edition of Johnson's work and greatly abridged.

1921.

57. Another issue of the above, but with title reading "Eleven Gower Street in / the County of London by Jonathan Cape / " instead of "Stationers' Hall Court," etc. "Reissued by Jonathan Cape, 1921 / All rights reserved / " on verso of title. Measurements, signatures and pagination the same as 1913 edition.

1922.

58. Another issue of the English (1913) edition, but with title reading "New York: / Robert M. McBride and Company / 1922 /," instead of, "Published at Stationers' Hall Court," etc. "First American Edition. Printed in the United States of America " appears in centre of verso of title-page, and "Printed in Great Britain by Billing and Sons, Ltd., Guildford & Esher," at the foot of same. It would appear to have been printed from the English plates.

All three editions have decorated yellow board covers, black cloth backs with white paper labels.

1921.

59. HISTOIRE / DES / PIRATES ANGLAIS / Depuis leur Etablissement dans l'Ile / de la Providence jusqu'à présent. / Contenant toutes leurs Aventures, Pirateries, Meurtres, / Cruautés, Excès, etc. . . / Avec / La Vie et les Aventures / De deux Femmes Pirates / Marie Read et Anne Bonny / traduit de l'Anglais / du Capitaine Charles Johnson / sur l'édition de 1774 / Preface de Pierre MacOrlan / (*printer's device*) / Paris / L'Edition Française Illustrée / 30, Rue de Provence /

Octavo.   The present copy measures $7\frac{1}{4}$ ins. by $4\frac{5}{8}$ ins.

Pagination.—Half-title p. (1): Histoire des Pirates Anglais, p. (2) frontispiece, title, p. (4) certificate of the number of the edition and copyright notice, preface pp. (5) to 8, pp. (9) to 253, p. (254) blank, list of contents pp. (255) and 256.

Published in wrappers printed in green and black, bearing an abbreviation of the title and a design of a pirate and the Jolly Roger, in the Collection Littéraire des Romans d'Aventures, in 1921.

1925.

60. A GENERAL / HISTORY / OF THE / PIRATES / *double rule* / By Captain Charles Johnson / Edited, with a Preface, by Philip Gosse / Adorned with Cuts by Alexina Ogilvie. / *double rule* / 19 / *(ornament)* / 25 / *double rule* / Kensington: Printed & sold by Philip Sainsbury / at The Cayme Press, Stanhope Mews West. /

Quarto. The present copy measures $11\frac{1}{4}$ ins. by $9\frac{3}{4}$ ins.

Signatures.—A to Q in fours, R (1 leaf), (signature marks K and N omitted).

Pagination.—Half-title, verso blank, title, preface pp. (v) to viii, pp. (1) to 130.

The verso of title-page bears the following: " *This edition of Johnson's General History of The Pirates has been set by hand at The Cayme Press ; it is strictly limited to 500 copies, 50 being for presentation and review.*"

A reprint of the third edition (1725), but omitting preface and introduction.

Published in black cloth with gothic lettering in gilt on back, " General / History / of the / Pirates / Johnson / I /". The sides bear a reproduction of a piece-of-eight in gilt. The title is within a double line border.

Actual year of publication 1926.

Volume II. of this edition will be published during 1927.

1926.

61. THE COMPLETE NEWGATE CALENDER / Being / Captain Charles Johnson's General History of the Lives / and Adventures of the Most Famous Highwaymen, Murderers, Street-Robbers and Account of the Voyages and Plunders of the Most Notorious / Pyrates, 1734; Captain Alexander Smith's Compleat / History of the Lives and Robberies of the Most Notorious Highwaymen, / Foot-Pads, Shop-Lifts and Cheats, 1719; The Tyburn Chronicle, 1768; / The Malefactor's Register, 1796; George Borrow's Celebrated Trials, 1825; The Newgate Calendar, by Andrew Knapp and William Baldwin, 1826; Camden Pelham's / Chronicles of Crime, 1841; etc. / Collated and edited with some appendices / by / J. L. Rayner / and / G. T. Crook / Volume one / London: Privately Printed for the Navarre / Society Limited, 23 New Oxford Street, W.C. 1. / MCMXXVI. /

Demy octavo. The present copy measures $8\frac{5}{8}$ ins. by $5\frac{5}{8}$ ins.

The work is in five volumes, each of about 330 pp. with engraved frontispieces and four or five engraved plates.

Johnson's work is scattered through the five volumes, and several " Lives " are omitted.

Published in black cloth, with gilt lettering and decoration on back in gilt.

1926.

62. A GENERAL / HISTORY / OF THE / ROBBERIES AND MURDERS / OF THE MOST NOTORIOUS / PIRATES / from their first rise and settlement in the / Island of Providence to the present year / By / Captain Charles Johnson / Edited by / Arthur L. Hayward / London / George Routledge & Sons, Ltd. / 1926 /

Octavo.   Present copy measures 9¾ ins. by 7¼ ins.

Signatures.—1 to 37 in eights, 38 (6 leaves).

Pagination.—Title, editor's note p. v, glossary of terms regarding " The old sea-going craft " p. vi, preface pp. vii to xiv, list of illustrations pp. xv and xvi, introduction pp. 1 to 21, p. 22 blank, pp. 23 to 603, p. (604) blank.   There is a frontispiece and 15 illustrations.   They are mostly reproductions from the engraved plates of the early editions, and include 3 from the Dutch translation, 1725, and a facsimile of the title-page of the first edition, 1724.   On p. 143 is printed an " Outline map of the Guinea Coast of Africa (inset Madagascar &c.)," and on p. 503 an " Outline map showing some of the principal haunts of the Pirates in the West Indies."

The book is reprinted from the fourth edition, two volumes, 1726.   It does not include a reproduction of the folding frontispiece " Map of the Middle Part of America " which appeared in the original second volume.

Published in black buckram with gilt lettering and design of skull and cross-bones on back.

1926.

63. An American issue of the last, published by Messrs. Dodd, Mead and Co.

1926.

64. THE / HISTORY / OF THE / LIVES AND BLOODY EXPLOITS / OF THE MOST / NOTED PIRATES; / THEIR / TRIALS AND EXECUTIONS. / Including A Correct Account Of The / Late Piracies / Committed In The West Indies, And The Expedition Of / Commodore Porter; Also, Those Committed / On The Brig Mexican, Who Were Tried / And Executed At Boston, in 1835. / (*rule*) / Embellished with Engravings from Original Designs. / (*rule*) / Empire State Book Company / New York / MCMXXVI /

Octavo.   The present copy measures $8\frac{9}{16}$ ins. by $5\frac{5}{8}$ ins.

No signatures.

Pagination.—Title, verso bearing " A Faithful Reprint of an Old Time Book," contents p. (1), p. (2) blank, list of illustrations p. (3), p. 4 blank, pp. (5) to 295, p. (296) blank. Pp. 5 to 250 is Johnson's " History." There are a frontispiece and eight illustrations.

The book is apparently a reprint of the Hartford, Ct., 1836 edition.   Published in orange colour cloth with black lettering on back, and front cover.   The latter also bears a black line border.

ADDENDA.

1726.

7*a*. HISTOIRE / DES / PIRATES / ANGLOIS, / Depuis leur Etablisse-
ment dans l'Isle de / la Providence, jusqu'à present. / Contenant toutes
leurs Avantures, Pi- / rateries, meurtres, cruautez & excès. / Avec / la Vie
et les Avantures / de deux Femmes Pirates, / Marie Read & Anne
Bonny. / Et un Extrait des Loix & des Ordonnantes / concernant la
Piraterie. / Traduite de l'Anglois du Capitaine / Charles Johnson. /
Premiere edition. / (*ornament*) / A Londres, / chez Jacob Walter,
Imprimeur / & Libraire, près Weminster. / MDCCXXVI.

Octavo. The present copy measures 6 ins. by $3\frac{3}{10}$ ins.

Signatures.—(a) to Ii in eights and fours.

Pagination.—Title, introduction pp. (i) to lvi, pp. (1) to 382, followed
by one page of Table des chapitres.

1842.

39*a*. LIVES AND EXPLOITS / OF / THE MOST CELEBRATED
PIRATES / AND SEA ROBBERS. / (*short rule*) / By T. Douglas /
(*short rule*) / London: / Published by J. S. Pratt. / (*short rule*) /
MDCCCXLII.

32mo. Present copy measures 5 ins. by 3 ins.

Signatures.—(A) to V in eights.

Pagination.—Half-title, verso blank, title, verso blank, pp. (i) to
index vi, (7) to 320. There is a frontispiece between half-title and
title showing " engagement between the Bon Homme Richard and the
Serapis."

Note: No. 41, a very similar edition, has for frontispiece a picture
of " Soto leaving the Morning Star to her Fate."

Published in green cloth with gilt lettering on the back and the sides
blind stamped.

(*Circa*) **1865.**

48a. THE / HISTORY / AND / ADVENTURES, / OF / DARING
ROBBERIES, / COMMITTED / ON THE / HIGH SEAS, / BY
NOTORIOUS PIRATES. / (*short rule*) / York : / printed and
published by C. Croshaw, / Pavement. / (*short rule*) / Price sixpence.

12mo, present copy measures 6⅜ ins. by 4 ins.

Signatures.—(A) to C in sixes, some mis-lettered.

Pagination.—Title, verso blank, pp. (1) to 36. Coloured frontispiece
of " the Swallow man of War taking the Royal Fortune, Capt. Roberts,
the noted Pirate," etc.

This is a very abbreviated copy of eight of Johnson's " Lives."

(*Circa*) **1880.**

51a. THE / LIVES AND DARING DEEDS / OF / THE MOST
CELEBRATED / PIRATES AND BUCCANEERS, / OF ALL
COUNTRIES. / (*short rule*) / with numerous engravings. / (*short
rule*) / Philadelphia: / Geo. G. Evans, 439 Chestnut Street.

Octavo. The present copy measures 7$\frac{3}{10}$ ins. by 4⅘ ins.

Signatures.—In eights: numerals in no order.

Pagination.—Half title, verso blank, title, verso blank, contents,
p. 5, verso blank, pp. 7 to 288, followed by 22 pages of advertisements
of books published by G. G. Evans.

Coloured frontispiece of Robin Hood. Several crude engravings
from various sources.

Published in green cloth, lettered and stamped in gold on back,
plain stamping on sides.